Festival of Women Writers – My Turn

GARNETTE ARLEDGE

Singing Stars Press,

Milton, New York

Copyright © 2013 Garnette Arledge

All rights reserved.

Photographs by Elga Antonsen ©

ISBN-13: 978-0-936319-03-2

Singing Stars Press
18 Josies Path, Milton, NY 12547
845-795-3202
www.garnettearledge.com, Facebook & @100kLightauthor

ACKNOWLEDGMENTS

Hobart Book Village Festival of Women Writers
September 6 - 8, 2013

A weekend for all, celebrating and exploring the Work of Women Writers in and around the picturesque Northern Catskill Book Village of Hobart, New York

Breena Clarke and Cheryl Clarke,
of Blenheim Hill Books
Elda Stefani, Hobart International Bookport
Adams' Antiquarian Book Shop
Liberty Rock Books
Mysteries and More Bookshop
Paper Moon Bookbinding
Bibliobarn

The Nineteen Women Writers

www.hobartbookvillage.com
Twitter: @hobartbooks and on Facebook
HobartBookVillage

Gratitude to dear Elga Antonsen, for the front and back cover photographs taken at the Festival

MY TURN

How many of you write like JD Salinger? Mentally, only, raise your hand if you do.

I know I do – and have five books to prove it. Two were in the closet for ten and twenty years. Another took fifteen years to live and then came out only because a publisher offered a contract in a surprising way, taking another two years to publication. The fourth, which was prepaid by the Hawaiian Kahuna, I wrote, acted as agent and sold to a publisher at the huge Javits Center ABA – but that's because it was for the Hawaiian, not for me, a book for hire. The fifth, my first, is in revision and expansion.

So here's how Salinger did it. First novel, traditionally. *Catcher in the Rye* debuted to a whirlwind of fame and fortune. *Franny and Zooey* ten years later when I was an undergraduate. At the University of Maryland, many of the women on my hall were from New Jersey. They went wild over it. We read in a gulp *Raise High the Roofbeams, Carpenters;* then *For Esme with Love,* and *Nine Stories.* But NOTHING ELSE.

He had fame, money, and perhaps any partner he might have wanted with his first book. And then for the next 40-50 years was a recluse. Now he's dead. A film was released, September 6, 2013 with scads of famous people saying how much he meant to them. Shown on PBS in January, 2014. For after his death, manuscripts of four more novels and one non-fiction book came to light from his vault.

So we know what he was doing. He was writing, tucked away from fame, fortune and allurement in the backwoods of New England.

Decades ago I learned his parents were active in the Sri Ramakrishna-Vivekananda center in

New York City. After they died, he kept the family apartment just around the corner. Evidently considered one of the Swamis there a Vedanta mentor. So it seems Mr. Salinger was a meditator, a hidden spiritual guy, who perhaps also believed like I do that work can be meditation, can be spiritual. His fifth hidden book is on eastern mysticism, so obviously my speculation is confirmed by his legacy. But I didn't know that when I put one and one together to make One about his motives for privacy.

I like to think he had greater reasons, more than just liking solitude, to eschew the noise and allure of literary stardom. He was writer, not a bright light gadfly. Trying to do both killed the poet Dylan Thomas on a bar room floor. No, Salinger valued his privacy – for it has literary merit. In itself, the act of writing may be work for the world, provided the intent is in alignment with the highest good.

Like some of us who have spent a long time in beautiful mountains, hidden away, writing, believing creation of thought counts. Example: Think Peace. Think Snow. For thoughts fill the air, just as surely as do radio, cell phone and Twitter waves.

Focus has energy. We need to be focused to write – at least I do. So Salinger kept on writing, even as people wondered what he was doing.

I ask again: how many of you here write like Salinger? You write because you write. Because it is the best use of your life to write. Not til later to focus on selling the book. Not til later to promote. Not until you want the press pressing on your every word. But because you must write. Because writing, while often tedious, time consuming and hard, is what you must do.

And perhaps (all this Salinger stuff is speculation, for I do write fiction) – just my idea. You have stories bursting out of your pores, angels exhorting you in dreams, or maybe there is nothing else so compelling as a way of life: as to write. Write stories. Do the research. Listen to the characters as they unfold a plot. Gather your dewdrops into prose.

Write because your life is then filled with everything you want: discipline, order, adventure, satisfaction, angst, companionship, accomplishment, hard-hard-hard work. Writing is no joke, even the comedians say that. Some of the hardest tasks you ever set for yourself involve putting good words together.

But there's something even harder if you are a writer. And that's stepping away from your blood, tears and joy of getting it into a book – that is promoting it. I'm an extrovert. I made my living in journalism, public relations, advertising and sales. I could sell your book. Promote it. I did it for the Kahuna, and others. But for my own books – barely. Social media helps for it is one step away from begging. The sale's pitch. The hoop-la.

Not that I write like Salinger, I'm not claiming that – but I write like Salinger. In private, excluded, secluded. I write because writing is.

Following are some readings from my books.

Book One

Wise Secrets of Aloha

Synopsis: *The sacred art of LomiLomi techniques told and taught to me by Kahuna Harry Jim. He feels intuitively the present times call for Hawaii's ageless hands-on secrets for overcoming pain of mind, body and spirit. How the art of LomiLomi raises the Aloha Spirit with-in. Includes amazing and true personal stories of healings, starting with mine after deep personal tragedy. (Pages 150, Weiser's Books, 2007)*

I met Harry Jim, the healing Kahuna, at a LomiLomi workshop shortly after my spiritual partner was killed changing a tire on the New York Thruway. He was headed towards New Jersey as he had a Substance Abuse Counselling service, with clients waiting for him. I took his sudden, violent death very hard as they did. It was a year before the blood stains near the Newburgh exit weathered off. Then, during a LomiLomi workshop, I was on a massage table enjoying the gentle Aloha process. Kahuna Harry walked over and placed his super-sized hand on my belly just below the rib cage. Then, he said, "What's this?" and pressed, sinking that big hand deep. It felt like he might be manipulating my spine from the up-side. Then suddenly, he pulled his hand out, taking what felt like a large sack of pain in the release. It was the year-old grief from the sudden death. He said "People store their unresolved emotions in their bodies. The feelings they cannot deal with are pushed into the body. I worked with many, many Vietnam vets living in the jungle on the Big Island, carrying their grief and horror in their solar plexus. Get up, Garnette, you have released the grief."

I took a free breath, restored to my usual joy: "You need a book."

"I know, been trying to write one for ten years."

"You tell me your stories; I'll write for you. I'm an author." And the deal was made.

Excerpts from Wise Secrets

"Introduction: Calling the Wave.

"Ho'opaipai O Ke Nalu. Now! Ho, dear reader, call the wave to you so you may be in the Pu'a, the now, as you read, understand, and become one with the legendary Hawaiian Islands that are called truly, paradise. *Ho'opaipai. Aloha!* – Kahuna Harry Uhane Jim.

"Let's start easy. We really want you to move the energy in your body into harmony, happiness, and gratitude. So here's your flight ticket – you are welcome with Aloha to enter the realm of Hawaiian Temple LomiLomi with Kahuna Harry Uhane Jim, initiated priest of the traditional mysteries of Hawaii. And what is Temple LomiLomi? Your questions will be answered as the waves of understanding flow into you.

"In this book you will learn about hands-on healing and the sacred flow of Hawaiian words. Words carrying healing, mystery, beauty, and spiritual depth. Words have power. Let's start with the traditional chant of the surfers that open this book: *Ho'opaipai O Ke Nalu*, call the wave. It is both a surrender to the mighty Pacific and a command flying gloriously over it, calling for the perfect wave for surfing to roll in.

Ho'opaipai O Ke Nalu.

"Show up perfect wave, please.

"So I can meet you. So I can be receiving."

"Chapter One: The Esoteric Aloha Spirit, p. 11:

"A Ke Akua! By your power and agreement, I declare: Open the Port. – Ancient Hawaiian invocation.

"Welcome to Hawaii, where every leaf, every rock, every person, every waterfall, the waves, the ocean, the beach, the scented trade winds, and all life is a manifestation of divine energy and brimming with *Aloha* for you.

"In this place, this space, the reigning idea is that, as God sees us, no one is above the other. Hawaiians see God in every form, and in no form is there not God's presence. Hawaii's secret of paradise is *Aloha*: "the breath of God is in our presence."

"*Aloha*, the beloved greeting for hello and goodbye known the world over, is a many-leveled, truly multi-splendored healing sound all by itself. There is in all creation, in Aloha, a bigger, wider, more substantive presence of spirituality than we can, at the surface see or know.

"So say *Aloha* now to yourself. Savor *Aloha*, the traditional greeting. Generosity offers you a scented white-ginger lei. You are the welcomed guest. *Aloha* overflows with hospitality, flashes abundance, and offers beauty to all.

"Thus, each person honored with Aloha feels loved, feels welcomed, feels beauty, feels warmth, and therefore feels joy. Emotions swim with delight, healing occurs. The separation of strangers is replaced with the natural warmth of being loved, being supported.

"When the plane touches down in Honolulu, the tradition is that beauties rush forward gracefully, singing *Aloha*, and placing leis around the necks of newcomers . . . This ritual is designed to raise the vibration of the travel-weary newcomer . . . thus benefitting all, the islanders and the travelers."

Book Two

One Hundred Thousand Lights: a love song to India

Synopsis: *Leaving behind a two-timing fiancé and job-stealing colleague, carrying only her phone and a spiritual guidebook, a high-tech manager, 36, lands in South India. She is a lost soul troubled by her recent past life breaking into this life. Guided from one mystical experience to another, surrounded by newfound friendships, deep spiritual teachings and great love, she finds inside herself the real meaning of her name, Grace.* (Fiction, Pages 210, Singing Stars Books, 2012)

For forty years, since beginning the ancient practice of Hindu meditation, I was interested in traveling to South India.

Reading the lives of the spiritual women and men who dedicated themselves to the uniquely Indian highway to Self-realization, deepened my commitment. My buying and restoring the Woodrow Wilson house on Library Place in Princeton, NJ, furthered that interest. For I discovered the eldest daughter of Woodrow and Ellen Anxson Wilson lived her final years in India, quoted in a *New York Times* article has having found "perfect peace." Perfect peace of mind, emotions, and of course, the body, also called me as I read her letters as I also studied countless teachings from swamis and yogic masters there. This novel is based on the four-months of travel journals I kept when I finally went there in 1993. Only the spiritual experiences are mine. The rest is plot as sitting with one's eyes closed does not have the action and intricacies of characterization a novel hopefully does. While Mike and Grace are completely fictional, not based on anyone I know, I came to love them and their love story, rambunctious as they are, 21st century hi-tech corporate singles. I gave Grace some problems, (no, none of mine), for otherwise there would be no plot development. I gave her a hatred and fear of a certain group of people – fears that I wanted her to heal from. Heal not only her immediate past but fears carried over from her previous lives. India can do that for people. Reincarnation is a golden thread in Hindustani. My book is about how such wounds can be healed. So in honor of Margaret Wilson, I'll read aloud Grace's journey to Chennai and on to Pondicherry, one Margaret Wilson may have made in the 1930's. By the way, I use the ancient/new names of places and cities restored by the Indians to back before the British altered them. Also, I am grateful to one reviewer who recognized the immense amount of research this novel entailed.

Chapter 7 Pondi Bus

"Dawn, chattering of the monkeys skittering along her front balcony, wakes Grace. Her hand moves automatically to find it is just minutes before she's to meet Niles for breakfast at Ramana Maharshi Ashram (in Tiruvannamalai) then grab the bus to Puducherry. Pondi, Niles calls it, like an old friend. Formerly French Pondicherry.

"She snaps off the mobile, stuffs it along with clothes, tooth and hair brushes into her replacement backpack, bravely bargained for in the teeming bazaar yesterday. Grabs bottled water and runs out among the monkeys. She's been avoiding their sharp fruit-eating teeth, their little white hands imploring, plucking, demanding from her. Now she startles them, as they startle her, and all dash in opposite directions.

Niles, finished with his *idlies*, plucks a bumpy-skinned yellow fruit and two bananas on his way out the door, pushing a hungry Grace away from the food. She is pulled along in his footsteps. Niles complains, 'We don't want to be on a local bus, but go directly to Chennai (Madras) then to Pondi,' as he strides on, leaving her to follow him. In the taxi from the ashram as they go by the Shiva Temple, Grace calls silently to Yogi Ramsuratkumar (YRSK)

'Please smooth the way and don't let me be lost in India, please, please, with this peculiar guy.' (To Audience: Niles is a minor character who misses the point of spiritual adventures.)

Grace's Cyber Journal

"Suddenly, inexplicably, the taxi stops. Now Niles wants to be introduced to the yogi. I cannot say no. Who am I to deprive someone of a yogic blessing? But it's a lesson: don't talk so much seems like bragging, one-upping with the latest guru, like those women on the holy Arunachala Mountain.

"At the session, YRSK is the same, as yesterday as he will be tomorrow. As I enter with Niles, one of the regulars whispers, KRIPA! My name in Sanskrit. They buzz softly to each other. Have I done something wrong letting Niles tag along? Is it 'invitation only' to this saint?

"Yet YRSK is so patient with the long queue waiting for his blessing/darshan. First there was a prosperous woman wanting him to arrange an interview with the Holy Man Sri Sathya Sai

Baba at Puttaparthi. Then a mother comes in with a very sulky teenage daughter. The mother explained this girl will be doing her exams. The yogi responds: 'Why bring her, woman? She needs to study. Let her study.'

"Then he looks at the student. 'You will do well,' he says it many, many times like a mantra, repeating it, patting her right arm, giving her rock candy, puffing tobacco smoke at her, peering into her eyes to see beyond the visible. To see, and arrange, the good outcome for her. Then, kindly, he says, 'Go home, study, you will do well.' To the mother, he says, 'Take her home, she needs to study.' This is one of the yogi's ways for putting power into the outcome. He indicates they can leave, and after prostrating to him, they do. The girl beams, mother, content with the blessing, ignores the reprimand for she has gotten what she wants.

"As they leave, so does an orange-sari clad woman, who departs in a huff because it seems to her, he did not 'help' the student. She did not understand. Instead reacting to YRSK's smoking and the appearance of his tiny dwelling, that pile of debris there for mystic reasons known only to YRSK. Hidden saints who disguise themselves for reasons only God knows. YRSK calls himself neither guru nor yogi but 'this beggar', while the orange clad woman calls herself 'swami' and had her mind set on appearances, hence pride in her new sari, and misses the *kripa*. (Kripa is the Sanskrit word for Grace.)

"Then, seemingly out of nowhere, YRSK looks at me, saying, "You can come back Friday." And gives me a yellow and red apple – no more grape tests and now I even have breakfast. So blissful. Why did I spend any time worrying? I have his Father's Blessings.

"Outside, in the dust next to the ancient Shiva Temple, Niles winks. We bow and walk through the market-mass of bodies to the bus station. It's Wednesday, two days in Pondicherry for Margaret Woodrow Wilson – confirmed and blessed."

Book Three

On Angels' Eve:

Making the most of your final time together

Synopsis: *Few of us are adequately prepared to say 'Good-bye' to loved ones who are about to pass out of sight, die. As human beings, our sense of grief and impending loss take hold of us, yet the final months, weeks, years spent with those we love can - and should - be one of support, comfort and love. As a Hospice Chaplain and spiritual mentor, Garnette Arledge, M.Div., has helped hundreds of people through this time of passage which she refers to as 'Angel's Eve.' She has taught children, parents, partners and friends - the angels of those who are dying - to fill their last moments with caring, love and memories. Now, in this unique guidebook, Garnette Arledge clearly explains how to make the most of this time together."* (Self-Help. Pages 250,

Square One Publishers, 2004)

I will just say that I wrote this book to help and support people as they rally around their dying loved ones in 2000 before 9/11. I wrote it before my partner Christopher died on the highway. He would not read it. Perhaps ... well, who knows why he didn't need it. And I couldn't be there for him being at home in Kingston, New York, asleep when he died.

After all the practical guidance in the book, I conclude with imagination. For that creative tool is all we really know about what happens after death of the body.

Conclusion of the book, page 219, Excerpt:

"As the Jedi-master Yoda famously said to Luke Skywalker, 'No try. Do.' Do rise from despair and look dying straight in the eyes, for you can conquer fears. Don't try. Do. Do rise from despair. Yes, dying is disturbing, it is difficult work, but it is not dark. Once we realize that, then 'Go to the Light' becomes the refrain you say at the end. Go to the Light. (NOTE: I said this to the air after the police left, informing me of the Christopher's death on the Thruway hours earlier. There was nothing else I could do, even with all my Hospice training. Yet, perhaps this too may be helpful to others hearing of a sudden death. Back to reading from book.)

"Here's a fable: The Butterfly Women.

"In an ancient culture, perhaps mythological, there were women in the remote villages who were called Butterflies. They had extraordinary abilities recognized from birth. For these extra-sighted girls could see the thin places between the highest sky and the Earth. As small children, the parents gave the girls' schooling to wise forest women, in order to train the girls as guides to the dying. For in this long-ago and far-away place, no one died alone.

"The Butterfly as friend and companion, sat by the bedside of a dying one. As the last lingering breaths slowly faded from the body, the soul would unbind gently and rise away, accompanied by a Butterfly. Together they would cross the bar, passing through the veil, and reach the beloved one's own clear, light place.

"Now, we may say that loved ones who die merely return to their energetic home, coming back to Earth at times, for special purposes only, but what do we know about the Great Mystery? Death and what happens after death are still a mystery. We leave that piece of what happens in the after-life as the great reward for living and dying. As my own beloved used to say when he heard someone had died, 'Wow, is he going to be surprised!'

"The Butterfly's role was to go with the soul, settle him into the next right place where he was most harmonious, and then return to Earth alone in order to tell those left behind exactly who, what, where, why and how it all occurred. These are the questions asked by those who remain. No one seems to know for sure.

"Only the wild butterflies know. Nature knows. Watch their cycle carefully. They start out looking like worms. Like we may feel sometimes. But they are really caterpillars, eating leaves for glory. When they have consumed everything they possibly can, they spin a cocoon-shroud around themselves. It looks like they have died. But no, after some time, the cocoon falls away, it's their Angel's Eve, and behold, a beautiful winged creature flies forth. We call them butterflies, I wonder what the Author of Creation calls them?

"Your Butterfly is waiting for you. Take her hand, she knows the way. For in the end poetry is the great solace."

Book Four

Night of the Mothers: when four magi follow their star

Synopsis: *Recent biblical scholarship speculates the Magi short story was a much later addition to The Gospel of Matthew. In my fantasy, I changed gender and number: four magi, all women, with wisdom teachings as gifts. Added spice with characters representing existing religions: Celtic, Buddhism, Hinduism, Zoarastrism, Greek, Roman, African (heir of the Queen of Sheba) and Judaism all coming to support Elizabeth birthing John the Baptist, plus her younger cousin Mary's child's birth. Only King Herod the Great, died 6 BCE, and his first wife Doris, are historically verifiable. Further, this is a time travel novel, back and forth to 9/11 for the parallels of archetypal birth and consequences.* (Pages 207. Fiction. Singing Stars Books. 2013)

Once upon a time, there were novels called *The Robe, Shoes of the Fisherman, Ben Hur* and from 1917, *Mary* by Sholem Asch, a powerful novel. Novelizations of the Christian Bible were heroic attempts in the 20th Century. Now in the post-church era, we are permitted to imagine and fill out the brief words. For example, in seminary, we were taught that the story of the Three Magi was a later insert and probably untrue so I felt I had been given a *carte blanche* for improvisation.

Then I noticed these twelve verses are a plot outline. I started with a riff, a speculation of 'what if?' beyond dogma, into story. So, I changed the Magi to four women midwives because I have a poetic license to go along with my pilot's license, now expired, to write whatever I like – also in the 20th Century Einstein said: 'time is a river.' So I added time travel which the Biblical writers did not address. The date authorities now posit Jesus' birth was 6 BCE (Before Common Era, no longer BC and AD, now BCE and CE but don't be concerned only scholars are paying attention to the change).

Further, as I first worked on the Magi novel, 9/11 burst on us, which to me was also biblical. If a book is about one time, it must be about all times. I saw the parallels of the ancient family being one human family. Herod was an Arab. So were Abraham, Isaac, Moses and Zechariah, Elizabeth, Mary and Joseph. Jesus. Not Muslims, none of them. As Mohammed lived six hundred plus years later. They were all Semitic, all inter-related by blood and marriage. So both Hebrew Bible and the Christian Bible are both testaments, as they said in seminary, of a long family saga. I've continued that theory, as these characters time travel, learning the hard, long way to love one another.

My inspiration for the novel came one morning. I thought then writing this poem was enough:

Indra's Net, (Poem, 1996)

One Sunday morning I had an epiphany in the early light.

It was the silent voice of the air as I was drying my long hair,

Determined not to go to church. "You were there."

"Me! How could this be?"

"You were a thread in Jesus' cloak.

His mother wove you into the Son's seamless garment.

You were a long strand of lamb's wool, blanched in the hot sun, to whiteness, combed, carded, and spun with brothers and sisters.

Then the Mother in her meditation at the loom, wove the idea of us with her shuttle, pulling weft through warp.

No beginning, no ending to the weaving.

We were a thought in Mary's mind, she manifested us into a cloak for Her Son.

A good plain garment.

We were with Jesus as he walked.

We kept him dry. We kept him warm. We were there when the Roman's cast lots as he hung dying.

We rose with him, trampled in his blood and dust.

We live still, woven into the fabric of Beingness.

Listen and you can hear this message in the looms of all thought, woven into the energy of Life Eternal.

Take care what you think, wearing the Cloth of Everlasting Life, All One."

Ninety thousand words later, it became this novel, Night of the Mothers.

Excerpt from Chapter Eight:

"And King Herod sent the Magi to Bethlehem, and said, Go search diligently for the young child, and when ye have found him, bring me word again, that I may come and worship him also - Matthew 2:8

"Away from crowded Bethlehem with its dangers from Herod and Rome, the Greek dancer Aha outran Natalie and Emilius tracing their path through the new life on the desert. She saw Maximilian racing towards them on his Roman charger. He pulled up, astonishment mirroring theirs but for a different reason, dismounted. 'Our Mary is here.'

"'Yes, Mary must be, love clears the way. Just look at the desert unwinding from winter.'"
"Arriving breathlessly, Emilius (son of Joseph of Arimathea) pounds Maximilian on the back, saying: "The Mother?" Natalie joins them, the serenity of her ancestor The Queen of Sheba, on her glistening face. Emilius said: 'Max, shall we

go to Mother Elizabeth's?'

'Yes. Though, that might make it difficult for you, Aha, with Lady Doris, Herod's spy there.'

"They settled down on the turf to plan. Max continued, 'We cannot rush in like angels when the plans have been held so secret and meticulous . . .'

"'But,' Emilius said, 'we must be there. My heart is aching and dancing at the same time, how I long for the Mary's glance, her touch.'

(Author aside: There is speculation 'Mary' may be a title rather than a personal name so many women carried it.)

"Aha and Natalie look at each other, both disciplined priests, wary of Emilius unbridled enthusiasm. "Emilius, you do see that we must protect the Mother's safety, we take care her.'

"'Yes, yes, of course, I do. But when will we see her? She's so close now.'

"While they considered, Natalie brought out the bag Abigail provided. Crusty bread, bites of fresh cheese, dried figs enough to share with

Maximilian. They ate sparingly, savoring the food and fresh air, then as healthy bodies who had been up all night meditating, they fell into deep, peaceful sleep. A cloak of peace played over them who still had much to learn.

"Aha awoke gradually, realizing slowly just where she was. On either side as if in their own nests like landbirds, her companions slept peacefully. Aha crossed her arms behind her head, looked into the arc of the heavens above. Clear, vast deeply blue daylight soared on forever — in the eastern quadrant, ghostly white sliver of moon— dark would bring it alive with Venus above its smile. Fragrance of the Earth surrounded her like perfume. Bees emerged from winter hives.

"The desert was alive with bees, flirting in ecstasy among the sudden unsheathing. Aha thought of Elizabeth so near now to the birth, Mary as her attendant. The two wise women sewing swaddling cloth and babe clothes in serenity, while at the same time angels wove the fabric of the air. Would the domestic heaven be spoiled by Herod, by Doris?

"Aha wondered how Mary and Elizabeth would deal with her encamped right in their midst. Would Doris, Herod's first wife and kin, be isolated to her room like the penitent she surely should be? Or would it be best for the normal flow of the household going on, with secret meetings, cautious words when Doris is out of the way, or maybe only in dark of night?

"Would Doris's presence deny them the grace of the Mothers' company? Then she discarded the idle thought as selfish. But surely it would not be right for a desperate Doris to know about those called forth and our plans?

"'I vow Doris shall not poison the air nor threaten the impending births of both babies with her wiles. We must take care of the Mothers.' And despite the miracle of the rebirth of spring, Persephone's return from Hades to her mother Demeter, Aha's jaw tightened in her self-righteousness, in her concern to protect the Holy Ones.

"So deep was she in her thoughts, Aha merely twitched the bee away that was tickling her. It dove again, buzzing her ear, so she batted it away with impatient hand. She turned over in the long grass to remove her ear, its target, only to see with surprise Maximilian's weather-beaten face, with its bold smile. He was wielding a fuzzy-wuzzy and laughing without guile at her. "Where were you? The expression on your face is fearsome."

"'Pest,' Aha could hardly respond to his playfulness so deep in the grip of worry and scheming thoughts. 'I was thinking of the Mothers' safety; you're the Roman soldier, what plan have you come up with to save them?'

"Maximillian puffed up his chest in mock authority, trying to look stern. 'Come, Aha, let the others' sleep, come away and we will plot and plan.' Aha rose cautiously, sandals crunching on the Earth, walking away from the area where Natalie and Emilius were still soundly at rest. They looked so young, lying in the tawny field, yet although they were in mid-teens they were all full working members of society.

'Max took her browned hand, and with his other raised a finger to smoothen the worry lines on Aha's face. 'You are forgetting one thing, my friend. WE don't take care of the Mothers. They take care of us. The Mother does not want us to plan or scheme. She is one with God. We need her but she surely does not need us to protect her. God is safe from attack, God cannot be attacked or diminished by anything we can say or do. Doris, Herod, Rome cannot harm her. Us, maybe they can hurt, with our ill-advised if well-meant schemes but not her, she is the Feminine Face of God on Earth.'

I have these same characters in a parallel situation in New York City at 9/11.

Conclusion of Festival Talk

If Salinger had the freedom, anonymity of Self-Publishing, would he have done that instead of stockpiling his work? I mean, authors write in solitude for sure, but for an audience. Without readers, why write? We are writing for each other, and I think that's what this Festival of Women Writers is about ultimately. He was a lone wolf – that's not woman's way – we make family, we make friends, we make community. We touch each other's hearts and souls on purpose.

I thank Breena Clarke and Cheryl Clarke, of Blenheim Books and Elda Stefani of the Hobart International Bookport for noticing I'm a writer and including me with this fabulous gathering of women – and I thank you for listening to me while I'm still alive.

What Jane Austen missed – knowing how she touched her readers. Still touches. Thank you.

For More Information:

Facebook: Garnette Arledge, Novelist and Writing Mentor

Twitter: @100kLightauthor

Web:
www.garnettearledge.com

Email:
aloha.garnette@gmail.com